MUNCHIES

Publications International, Ltd.

Photograph on front cover copyright © Shutterstock.com.

Pictured on the front cover: Buffalo Wings *(page 126)* and Sweet Soy Ginger Chicken *(page 120).*

Pictured on the back cover *(clockwise from top):* Chorizo Quesadillas *(page 70),* Quick Waffled Quesadillas *(page 58)* and Mozzarella Sticks *(page 130).*

ISBN: 978-1-64558-251-9

Manufactured in China.

8 7 6 5 4 3 2 1

Microwave Cooking: Microwave ovens vary in wattage. Use the cooking times as guidelines and check for doneness before adding more time.

Let's get social!
@Publications_International
@PublicationsInternational
www.pilbooks.com

TABLE OF Contents

Snacks
FOR BINGING

EASY-ISH SNACKS TO MAKE IN THE MIDDLE OF THE NIGHT, OR ANY TIME YOU NEED QUICK AND TASTY SNACKING OPTIONS.

GARLIC BREAD WAFFLE STICKS

Makes 5 to 6 servings

2 cloves garlic, minced

¼ teaspoon kosher salt

¼ cup grated Parmesan cheese

3 tablespoons butter, melted

2 tablespoons finely chopped fresh parsley

2 cans (8 ounces each) refrigerated crescent dough

Marinara sauce, heated

1. Preheat classic square waffle maker to medium-high heat.

2. Place garlic on cutting board; sprinkle with salt. Using tip of chef's knife, press salt into garlic until it forms smooth paste. Transfer paste to medium bowl; stir in cheese, butter and parsley.

3. Unroll dough. Arrange dough edge-to-edge onto waffle maker to fill entire cooking surface, cutting pieces as needed to fit.

4. Close lid; cook about 2 minutes or until golden brown. Open lid; brush top of waffle with garlic butter. Close lid; cook 30 seconds. Remove to wire rack. Repeat with remaining dough.

5. Cut into sticks. Serve with marinara sauce.

BBQ CHICKEN RAMEN PIZZAS

MAKES 2 SERVINGS

1 package (3 ounces) ramen noodles, any flavor*

¼ cup barbecue sauce

½ cup chopped cooked chicken

2 tablespoons chopped green onion

¼ cup (1 ounce) shredded Cheddar cheese

Discard seasoning packet.

1. Preheat oven to 400°F. Line baking sheet with foil. Break noodles in half into two flat pieces. Place on prepared baking sheet. Bake noodles 4 minutes to lightly toast.

2. Spread barbecue sauce over noodles. Layer chicken and green onion on sauce; sprinkle with cheese.

3. Bake 4 minutes or until cheese melts and noodles begin to brown.

EVERYTHING SEASONING DIP WITH BAGEL CHIPS

MAKES ABOUT 2 CUPS DIP (ABOUT 16 SERVINGS)

2 large bagels, sliced vertically into rounds

1 container (12 ounces) whipped cream cheese

1½ tablespoons finely chopped green onions (green parts only)

1 teaspoon dried minced onion

1 teaspoon granulated garlic

1 teaspoon sesame seeds

1 teaspoon poppy seeds

¼ teaspoon kosher salt

Sliced green onions (green parts only)

1. Preheat oven to 350°F. Line baking sheet with parchment paper or leave ungreased. Place bagel rounds on prepared baking sheet.

2. Bake 10 to 12 minutes or until golden brown, shaking occasionally.

3. Meanwhile, combine cream cheese, chopped green onions, minced onion, garlic, sesame seeds, poppy seeds and salt in medium bowl until well blended. Garnish with sliced green onion. Serve with bagel chips.

CHOCOLATE-COVERED BACON
MAKES 12 SLICES

12 slices thick-cut bacon

12 wooden skewers (12 inches)

1 cup semisweet chocolate chips

2 tablespoons shortening, divided

1 cup white chocolate chips or butterscotch chips

1. Preheat oven to 400°F. Thread each bacon slice onto wooden skewer. Place on rack in large baking pan. Bake 20 to 25 minutes or until crisp. Cool completely.

2. Combine semisweet chocolate chips and 1 tablespoon shortening in large microwavable bowl. Microwave on HIGH at 30-second intervals until melted and smooth.

3. Combine white chocolate chips and remaining 1 tablespoon shortening in large microwavable bowl. Microwave on HIGH at 30-second intervals until melted and smooth.

4. Drizzle chocolates over each bacon slice as desired. Place on waxed paper-lined baking sheets. Refrigerate until firm. Store in refrigerator.

NACHOS
MAKES 8 SERVINGS

48 tortilla chips

2 teaspoons olive oil

1 cup chopped onion

1 tablespoon chili powder

2 teaspoons dried oregano

1 can (about 15 ounces) pinto beans or black beans, rinsed and drained

2 tablespoons water

1¼ cups (5 ounces) shredded Monterey Jack cheese

¾ cup frozen corn, thawed and drained

1 jar (2 ounces) pimientos, drained

3 tablespoons sliced pitted black olives

2 to 3 tablespoons pickled jalapeño pepper slices, drained

1. Preheat oven to 375°F. Place tortilla chips on large baking sheet.

2. Heat oil in medium saucepan over medium-high heat. Add onion; cook and stir about 5 minutes or until tender. Add chili powder and oregano; cook and stir 1 minute. Remove from heat. Add beans and 2 tablespoons water; mash with fork or potato masher until blended but still chunky. Cover and cook over medium heat 6 to 8 minutes or until bubbly, stirring occasionally. Stir in additional water if beans become dry.

3. Sprinkle cheese evenly over chips. Spoon beans over chips. Combine corn and pimientos in small bowl; spoon over beans. Bake about 8 minutes or until cheese is melted. Sprinkle with olives and jalapeños.

PRETZEL DIPPERS

MAKES 48 PIECES

⅓ cup spicy brown mustard

3 tablespoons whipped butter

2 tablespoons mayonnaise

1 package frozen soft pretzels (6 pretzels)

24 thin slices salami, cut into halves

10 ounces Swiss cheese, cut into scant ½-inch cubes

1. Whisk mustard, butter and mayonnaise in small bowl until well blended.

2. Dampen pretzels with water and sprinkle with salt from package. Microwave according to package directions until pretzels are warm.

3. Cut each pretzel into 8 pieces. Wrap half slice of salami around each pretzel piece; top with cheese cube and secure with toothpick. Serve with mustard sauce for dipping.

INSIDE-OUT BREADSTICKS

MAKES 6 SERVINGS

1 package (about 11 ounces) refrigerated breadsticks (12 breadsticks)

1 package (8 ounces) cream cheese, softened

1 to 2 tablespoons milk

¼ cup finely chopped carrot

2 tablespoons minced fresh chives or green onions

12 slices deli ham, roast beef or turkey

1. Bake breadsticks according to package directions; cool.

2. Place cream cheese and 1 tablespoon milk in medium bowl; beat with wooden spoon until well blended and spreadable, adding additional milk if needed. Stir in carrot and chives.

3. Spread rounded tablespoon cream cheese mixture over each ham slice. Roll ham slices around breadsticks. Serve immediately or wrap in plastic warp and refrigerate until needed.

GUACAMOLE PLATTER

Makes 6 to 8 servings

4 ripe avocados

¼ cup fresh lime juice

2 tablespoons olive oil

3 cloves garlic, crushed

½ teaspoon salt

¼ teaspoon black pepper

1 cup (4 ounces) shredded Colby Jack cheese

1 cup diced seeded plum tomatoes

⅓ cup sliced pitted black olives

⅓ cup salsa

1 tablespoon minced fresh cilantro

Tortilla chips

1. Cut avocados in half; remove pits. Scoop pulp into large bowl. Add lime juice, oil, garlic, salt and pepper; mash to desired consistency.

2. Spread avocado mixture evenly on large plate or serving platter, leaving 1-inch border around edge. Top with cheese, tomatoes, olives, salsa and cilantro. Serve with tortilla chips.

QUICK THAI NOODLE WRAPS

MAKES 8 WRAPS

1 package (3 ounces) ramen noodles, any flavor*

2 teaspoons creamy peanut butter

1½ cups packaged shredded coleslaw mix

½ cup diced cooked chicken

8 (6-inch) flour tortillas

Soy sauce

Discard seasoning packet.

1. Cook noodles according to package directions; do not drain. Add peanut butter, 1 teaspoon at a time, stirring until melted. Stir in coleslaw mix and chicken; cover and set aside 2 minutes.

2. Spoon noodle mixture onto tortillas. Drizzle with soy sauce, if desired. Roll up and serve immediately.

MEXICAN FLATS

Makes 2 servings

2 (6-inch) corn tortillas

½ cup (2 ounces) shredded sharp Cheddar cheese

2 tablespoons sour cream

¼ cup canned black beans, rinsed, drained and lightly mashed with fork

¼ cup salsa

¼ cup sliced pitted black olives

1. Place tortillas on microwavable plates. Sprinkle ¼ cup cheese over each tortilla.

2. Cover each plate with waxed paper; microwave on HIGH 20 to 30 seconds or until cheese melts.

3. Carefully remove waxed paper. Spread 1 tablespoon sour cream over each tortilla. Top with beans, salsa and olives. Serve open-faced or fold in half.

MINI CHEESE DOGS

MAKES 32 MINI CHEESE DOGS

1 package (16 ounces) hot dogs (8 hot dogs)

6 ounces pasteurized process cheese product

2 packages (16 ounces each) jumbo homestyle buttermilk biscuits (8 biscuits per package)

1. Preheat oven to 350°F. Line baking sheet with parchment paper or spray with nonstick cooking spray.

2. Cut each hot dog into 4 pieces. Cut cheese into 32 (1×½-inch) pieces.

3. Separate biscuits; cut each biscuit in half. Wrap 1 piece of hot dog and 1 piece of cheese in each piece of dough. Place seam side up on baking sheet.

4. Bake 15 minutes or until biscuits are golden brown. Serve warm.

VEGGIE VARIATION

To make this snack vegetarian-friendly, substitute 8 veggie dogs (soy protein links) for the regular hot dogs. Veggie dogs can be found in the produce section (or sometimes the freezer section) of the supermarket.

MINI CHEESE BURRITOS
MAKES 4 SERVINGS

½ cup canned refried beans

4 (8-inch) flour tortillas

½ cup chunky salsa

4 (¾-ounce) Cheddar cheese sticks*

Or cut a block of Cheddar cheese into ½-inch sticks.

1. Spread beans over tortillas, leaving ½-inch border around edges. Spoon salsa over beans.

2. Place cheese stick on one side of each tortilla. Fold edge of tortilla over cheese stick; roll up. Place burritos, seam side down, in microwavable dish. Microwave on HIGH 1 to 2 minutes or until cheese is melted. Let stand 1 to 2 minutes before serving.

Snacks BY THE HANDFUL

DO YOUR FUTURE SELF A FAVOR AND MAKE A BIG BATCH OF YUMMY, CRUNCHY SNACK MIX TO ENJOY ANY TIME OF THE DAY OR NIGHT.

PARTY POPCORN

MAKES 6 QUARTS

¼ cup vegetable oil

½ cup unpopped popcorn kernels

1 teaspoon fine sea salt or popcorn salt

4 ounces almond bark,* chopped *or* 1 cup white chocolate chips

Rainbow nonpareils

Look for almond bark by the chocolate chips in the baking aisle of the grocery store.

1. Line two sheet pans with parchment paper.

2. Heat oil in large 6-quart saucepan over medium-high heat 1 minute. Add popcorn; cover tightly with lid. Cook 2 to 5 minutes or until popcorn slows to about 1 second between pops, carefully shaking pan occasionally.

3. Spread popcorn on prepared sheet pans; immediately sprinkle with salt and toss gently to blend.

4. Melt almond bark according to package directions. Drizzle over popcorn; sprinkle with nonpareils. Let stand until set.

CRUNCHY RAMEN CHOW

MAKES ABOUT 8 CUPS

4 packages (3 ounces each) ramen noodles, any flavor*

1 cup semisweet chocolate chips

1 cup butterscotch chips

¾ cup creamy peanut butter

¼ cup (½ stick) butter

1½ cups powdered sugar

*Discard seasoning packets.

1. Break noodles into ½-inch bite-size pieces; place in large bowl.

2. Combine chocolate chips, butterscotch chips, peanut butter and butter in medium microwavable bowl. Microwave on HIGH 1 minute; stir. Continue to microwave at 30-second intervals, stirring until smooth.

3. Pour chocolate mixture over noodles; toss to coat evenly.

4. Place powdered sugar in 1-gallon resealable food storage bag. Add noodle mixture; shake until well coated. Spread in single layer on waxed or parchment paper to cool. Store in airtight container.

PARMESAN RANCH SNACK MIX

MAKES ABOUT 9 CUPS

3 cups corn or rice cereal squares

2 cups oyster crackers

1 package (5 ounces) bagel chips, broken in half

1½ cups mini pretzel twists

1 cup shelled pistachio nuts

2 tablespoons grated Parmesan cheese

¼ cup (½ stick) butter, melted

1 package (1 ounce) dry ranch salad dressing mix

½ teaspoon garlic powder

1. Combine cereal, oyster crackers, bagel chips, pretzels, pistachios and cheese in large microwavable bowl; mix gently.

2. Combine butter, salad dressing mix and garlic powder in small bowl. Pour over cereal mixture; toss lightly to coat. Microwave on HIGH 6 minutes, stirring at 2-minute intervals.

3. Spread on large rimmed baking sheet; cool completely.

CINNAMON CARAMEL CORN

MAKES 4 SERVINGS

8 cups air-popped* popcorn (about ⅓ cup kernels)

2 tablespoons honey

2 tablespoons butter

¼ teaspoon ground cinnamon

¼ teaspoon salt

Or follow steps 1 and 2 on page 29, using 2 tablespoons vegetable oil and ⅓ cup unpopped popcorn kernels.

1. Preheat oven to 300°F. Spray large baking sheet with nonstick cooking spray. Place popcorn in large bowl.

2. Combine honey, butter, cinnamon and salt in small saucepan; cook and stir over low heat until butter is melted and mixture is smooth. Immediately pour over popcorn; toss to coat evenly. Pour onto prepared baking sheet.

3. Bake 12 to 14 minutes or until coating is golden brown and appears crackled, stirring twice.

4. Cool popcorn on baking sheet. (As popcorn cools, coating becomes crisp. If not crisp enough, or if popcorn softens upon standing, return to oven and heat 5 to 8 minutes.) Store in airtight container.

CAJUN POPCORN

Preheat oven and prepare baking sheet as directed above. Replace cinnamon with 1 teaspoon Cajun or Creole seasoning and add 1 extra teaspoon honey. Proceed with recipe as directed above.

APRICOT-PECAN SNACK MIX

Makes 16 servings

3 tablespoons butter

1 tablespoon lime juice

2 cups bite-size shredded wheat cereal

1 cup thinly sliced dried apricots

1 cup pecan halves

¼ cup packed brown sugar

1½ teaspoons chili powder

½ teaspoon salt

¼ teaspoon ground cumin

1. Preheat oven to 325°F. Line baking sheet with foil.

2. Melt butter in large saucepan over low heat. Stir in lime juice. Add cereal, apricots, pecans, brown sugar, chili powder, salt and cumin; cook and stir 3 minutes or until brown sugar is melted. Spread mixture on prepared baking sheet.

3. Bake about 12 minutes or until cereal is toasted, stirring halfway through. Cool completely on baking sheet on wire rack. Store in airtight container.

MISO POPCORN CRUNCH

MAKES ABOUT 6 CUPS

4 cups popped popcorn

1 package (3 ounces) ramen
    noodles, any flavor,
    crumbled*

1 cup cashews

2 tablespoons butter, melted

1 tablespoon miso paste

1 tablespoon water

Discard seasoning packet.

1. Preheat oven to 350°F. Line baking sheet with parchment paper. Combine popcorn, noodles and cashews in large bowl.

2. Combine butter, miso paste and water in small bowl. Pour over popcorn mixture; toss to coat. Spread mixture on prepared baking sheet.

3. Bake 10 minutes. Cool completely on baking sheet.

HOT BUTTERY NUTS

MAKES 4 CUPS

¼ cup (½ stick) butter

2 cloves garlic, crushed

1 cup pecan halves

1 cup shelled pistachios

1 cup whole cashews

½ cup whole almonds

½ to ⅔ cup canned onion rings or French fried onions

1 to 1¼ teaspoons chipotle chile powder*

½ teaspoon salt

½ teaspoon ground cumin

½ teaspoon smoked paprika

For milder flavor, use ¾ to 1 teaspoon; for more spiciness, use 1¼ teaspoons.

1. Preheat oven to 300°F. Melt butter in large heavy saucepan over low heat. Stir in garlic; remove from heat. Cover and let stand 5 minutes.

2. Remove garlic with slotted spoon. Add pecans, pistachios, cashews, almonds, onion rings, chipotle chile powder, salt, cumin and paprika; stir gently to coat nuts with butter and spices. Spread evenly on ungreased rimmed baking sheet.

3. Bake 16 to 20 minutes or until nuts are fragrant and golden brown, stirring after 10 minutes. Cool completely on baking sheet. Store in airtight container.

POPCORN GRANOLA

Makes 8 servings

1 cup quick oats

6 cups popped popcorn

1 cup golden raisins

½ cup chopped mixed dried fruit

¼ cup sunflower kernels

2 tablespoons butter

2 tablespoons packed brown sugar

1 tablespoon honey

¼ teaspoon ground cinnamon

¼ teaspoon ground nutmeg

Popcorn salt or other fine salt

1. Preheat oven to 350°F. Spread oats on ungreased baking sheet; bake 10 to 15 minutes or until lightly toasted, stirring occasionally.

2. Combine oats, popcorn, raisins, dried fruit and sunflower kernels in large bowl.

3. Heat butter, brown sugar, honey, cinnamon and nutmeg in small saucepan over medium heat until butter is melted. Drizzle over popcorn mixture; toss to coat. Sprinkle with salt to taste.

ROSEMARY NUT MIX

MAKES 4 CUPS

2 tablespoons butter

2 cups pecan halves

1 cup unsalted macadamia nuts

1 cup walnuts

1 teaspoon dried rosemary

½ teaspoon salt

¼ teaspoon red pepper flakes

1. Preheat oven to 300°F.

2. Melt butter in large saucepan over low heat. Stir in pecans, macadamias and walnuts. Add rosemary, salt and red pepper flakes; cook and stir about 1 minute. Spread mixture on ungreased baking sheet.

3. Bake 8 to 10 minutes, stirring occasionally. Cool completely on baking sheet on wire rack.

CRANBERRY GORP

MAKES ABOUT 6 CUPS

¼ cup (½ stick) butter

¼ cup packed brown sugar

1 tablespoon maple syrup

1 teaspoon curry powder

½ teaspoon ground cinnamon

1½ cups dried cranberries

1½ cups coarsely chopped walnuts and/or slivered almonds

1½ cups lightly salted pretzel nuggets

1. Preheat oven to 300°F. Lightly grease large baking sheet.

2. Combine butter, brown sugar and maple syrup in large saucepan; cook and stir over medium heat until butter is melted and mixture is smooth. Stir in curry powder and cinnamon. Add cranberries, walnuts and pretzels; stir until evenly coated.

3. Spread mixture on prepared baking sheet. Bake 15 minutes or until mixture is lightly browned. Cool completely on baking sheet. Store in airtight container.

CITRUS CANDIED NUTS

MAKES ABOUT 3 CUPS

1 egg white

1½ cups whole almonds

1½ cups pecan halves

1 cup powdered sugar

2 tablespoons lemon juice

2 teaspoons grated orange peel

1 teaspoon grated lemon peel

½ teaspoon salt

⅛ teaspoon ground nutmeg

1. Preheat oven to 300°F. Lightly grease large rimmed baking sheet.

2. Beat egg white in medium bowl with electric mixer at high speed until soft peaks form. Add almonds and pecans; stir until well coated. Stir in powdered sugar, lemon juice, orange peel, lemon peel, salt and nutmeg until evenly coated. Spread nuts in single layer on prepared baking sheet.

3. Bake 30 minutes, stirring after 20 minutes. Turn off heat. Let nuts stand in oven 15 minutes. Transfer nuts to sheet of foil. Cool completely. Store in airtight container up to 2 weeks.

CHOCO-PEANUT BUTTER POPCORN

MAKES ABOUT 8 CUPS

1 cup semisweet chocolate chips

6 tablespoons creamy peanut butter

2 tablespoons butter

8 cups popped popcorn

1 cup powdered sugar

1. Microwave chocolate chips, peanut butter and butter in large microwavable bowl on HIGH 30 seconds; stir. Microwave and stir at 30-second intervals or until melted and smooth.

2. Pour mixture over popcorn in large bowl, stirring until evenly coated. Transfer to 1-gallon resealable food storage bag.

3. Add powdered sugar to bag; seal bag. Shake until well coated. Spread onto waxed paper to cool. Store leftovers in airtight container in refrigerator.

PIZZA & Quesadillas

THERE'S NOTHING LIKE MELTY, CHEESY, GOOEY PIZZA AND QUESADILLAS TO SATISFY ANY SIZE SNACK ATTACK.

CHICKEN PESTO PIZZAS WITH SPINACH AND TOMATOES

MAKES 4 SERVINGS

1 large (12-inch) prepared pizza crust *or* 2 small (6-inch) crusts

⅓ cup pesto sauce

1 cup shredded or chopped cooked chicken

1 plum tomato, thinly sliced

½ cup baby spinach, coarsely chopped

1 cup (4 ounces) shredded mozzarella cheese

1. Preheat oven to 375°F.

2. Place crust on pizza pan or baking sheet. Spread pesto evenly over crust; layer evenly with chicken, tomatoes, spinach and cheese.

3. Bake 12 to 14 minutes or until cheese is melted and crust is golden brown.

CHIPOTLE CHICKEN QUESADILLAS

Makes 5 servings

1 package (8 ounces) cream cheese, softened

1 cup (4 ounces) shredded Mexican cheese blend

1 tablespoon minced canned chipotle pepper in adobo sauce

5 (10-inch) flour tortillas

5 cups shredded cooked chicken (about 1¼ pounds)

Optional toppings: guacamole, sour cream, salsa and chopped fresh cilantro

1. Combine cream cheese, Mexican cheese blend and chipotle pepper in large bowl; mix well.

2. Spread ⅓ cup cheese mixture over half of one tortilla. Top with about 1 cup chicken. Fold tortilla over filling and press gently. Repeat with remaining tortillas, cheese mixture and chicken.

3. Heat large nonstick skillet over medium-high heat. Spray outside surface of each quesadilla with cooking spray. Cook quesadillas 2 to 3 minutes per side or until lightly browned.

4. Cut each quesadilla into wedges. Serve with desired toppings.

BBQ CHICKEN FLATBREAD

MAKES 4 SERVINGS

3 tablespoons red wine vinegar

2 teaspoons sugar

¼ red onion, thinly sliced (about ⅓ cup)

3 cups shredded rotisserie chicken

½ cup barbecue sauce

1 package (about 14 ounces) refrigerated pizza dough

1½ cups (6 ounces) shredded mozzarella cheese

1 green onion, thinly sliced diagonally

2 tablespoons chopped fresh cilantro

1. Preheat oven to 400°F. Line baking sheet with parchment paper.

2. For pickled onion, combine vinegar and sugar in small bowl; stir until sugar is dissolved. Add red onion; cover and let stand at room temperature while preparing flatbread. Combine chicken and barbecue sauce in medium bowl; toss to coat.

3. Roll out dough into 11×9-inch rectangle on prepared baking sheet; top with cheese and barbecue chicken mixture.

4. Bake about 12 minutes or until crust is golden brown and cheese is melted. Drain red onion; sprinkle over flatbread. Garnish with green onion and cilantro. Serve immediately.

QUICK WAFFLED QUESADILLAS

MAKES 1 SERVING

2 (6-inch) flour tortillas

⅓ cup (1½ ounces) shredded Cheddar cheese or Monterey Jack cheese

¼ cup finely chopped poblano pepper or jalapeño pepper

1 small plum tomato, chopped

⅛ teaspoon ground cumin

Salt and black pepper

½ ripe medium avocado, chopped

1 to 2 tablespoons chopped fresh cilantro

Juice of ½ lime

1. Preheat classic round waffle maker to medium. Coat both sides of each tortilla with nonstick cooking spray.

2. Top one tortilla with cheese, poblano pepper, tomato and cumin. Season with salt and pepper. Top with other tortilla. Place on waffle maker; close, pressing down slightly. Cook 3 minutes or until golden brown and cheese is melted.

3. Carefully remove tortilla. Cut into quarters using a serrated knife. Top with avocado, cilantro and lime juice.

QUATTRO FORMAGGIO PIZZA

Makes 4 servings

½ cup prepared pizza or marinara sauce

1 (12-inch) prepared pizza crust

4 ounces shaved or thinly sliced provolone cheese

2 ounces Asiago or brick cheese, thinly sliced

1 cup (4 ounces) shredded smoked or regular mozzarella cheese

¼ cup grated Parmesan or Romano cheese

1. Preheat oven to 450°F. Spread pizza sauce evenly over pizza crust; place on baking sheet.

2. Sprinkle with provolone and Asiago cheeses; top with mozzarella and Parmesan cheeses. Bake 14 minutes or until crust is golden brown and cheeses are melted. Cut into wedges.

VEGETABLE-BEAN QUESADILLAS

Makes 8 servings

1 tablespoon canola oil

1 cup sliced onion

1 can (about 15 ounces) black beans, rinsed and drained

1 cup sliced green bell pepper

1 cup sliced red bell pepper

½ teaspoon salt

½ teaspoon ground cumin

¼ teaspoon ground red pepper

8 (8-inch) whole grain tortillas

1 cup (4 ounces) shredded Cheddar cheese

Salsa and sour cream (optional)

1. Heat oil in large nonstick skillet over medium-high heat. Add onion; cook and stir 2 minutes or until translucent. Add beans, bell peppers, salt, cumin and red pepper; cook and stir 3 minutes or until bell peppers are crisp-tender.

2. Heat medium nonstick skillet over medium heat. Place 1 tortilla in skillet. Spread about ⅓ cup vegetables on half of tortilla; sprinkle with 2 tablespoons cheese. Fold tortilla over filling and cook until light brown on bottom. Turn and brown other side. Fill and cook remaining tortillas. Cut into wedges. Serve with salsa and sour cream, if desired.

TORTILLA PIZZA WEDGES

Makes 4 servings

2 teaspoons olive oil

1 cup frozen corn, thawed

1 cup thinly sliced mushrooms

4 (6-inch) corn tortillas

¼ cup pasta sauce

1 to 2 teaspoons chopped jalapeño pepper

¼ teaspoon dried oregano

¼ teaspoon salt

½ cup (2 ounces) shredded mozzarella cheese

1. Preheat oven to 450°F. Heat oil in large skillet over medium heat. Add corn and mushrooms; cook and stir 4 to 5 minutes or until tender.

2. Place tortillas on baking sheet. Bake 4 minutes or until edges begin to brown.

3. Combine pasta sauce, jalapeño, oregano and salt in small bowl. Spread evenly over tortillas. Top evenly with corn and mushrooms. Sprinkle with cheese.

4. Bake 4 to 5 minutes or until cheese is melted and pizzas are heated through. Cut each pizza into four wedges.

BAKED BLACK BEAN QUESADILLAS

MAKES 2 TO 4 SERVINGS

4 (8-inch) flour tortillas

¾ cup (3 ounces) shredded Monterey Jack or Cheddar cheese

½ cup canned black beans, rinsed and drained

2 green onions, sliced

¼ cup chopped fresh cilantro

½ teaspoon ground cumin

Salsa and sour cream

1. Preheat oven to 450°F. Spray large baking sheet with nonstick cooking spray or line with foil. Place 2 tortillas on prepared baking sheet; sprinkle each with half the cheese.

2. Combine beans, green onions, cilantro and cumin in small bowl; mix lightly. Spoon bean mixture evenly over cheese; top with remaining tortillas. Spray tops with cooking spray.

3. Bake 10 to 12 minutes or until cheese is melted and tortillas are lightly browned. Cut into quarters; top each tortilla wedge with 1 tablespoon salsa and 1 teaspoon sour cream.

MEXICAN PIZZA

Makes 8 servings

1 package (about 14 ounces) refrigerated pizza dough

1 cup chunky salsa

1 teaspoon ground cumin

1 cup canned black beans, rinsed and drained*

1 cup frozen corn, thawed

½ cup sliced green onions

1½ cups (6 ounces) shredded Mexican cheese blend

½ cup chopped fresh cilantro (optional)

Save the remaining 3⁄4 cup beans (from a 15- or 16-ounce can) in the refrigerator for up to 4 days to add to salads or soups.

1. Preheat oven to 425°F. Spray large baking sheet with nonstick cooking spray. Unroll pizza dough on prepared pan; press dough evenly to all edges of pan. Bake 8 minutes.

2. Combine salsa and cumin in small bowl; spread over partially baked crust. Top with beans, corn and green onions.

3. Bake 8 minutes or until crust is golden brown. Top with cheese; continue baking 2 minutes or until cheese is melted. Cut into squares; garnish with cilantro, if desired.

CHORIZO QUESADILLAS
Makes 6 servings

1 package (9 ounces) pork or vegetarian chorizo

1 cup coarsely chopped cauliflower

1 small onion, finely chopped

12 (6-inch) flour tortillas

1½ cups (6 ounces) chihuahua cheese

6 teaspoons vegetable oil

Salsa, guacamole and sour cream

1. Heat medium skillet over medium-high heat. Add chorizo, cauliflower and onion; cook and stir 10 to 12 minutes or until cauliflower is tender. Transfer to bowl. Wipe out skillet.

2. Spread ¼ cup chorizo mixture onto each of 4 tortillas. Top with ¼ cup cheese and remaining tortillas.

3. Heat 1 teaspoon oil in same skillet over medium-high heat. Add one quesadilla; cook 2 to 3 minutes per side or until well browned and cheese is melted. Repeat with remaining oil and quesadillas. Cut into wedges; serve with salsa, guacamole and sour cream.

 **NOTE** To keep cooked quesadillas warm, arrange on a baking sheet and place in a preheated 200°F oven until all the quesadillas are cooked and ready to serve.

QUESADILLA GRANDE

Makes 1 to 2 servings

2 (8-inch) flour tortillas

2 to 3 large fresh stemmed spinach leaves or ½ cup baby spinach (optional)

2 to 3 slices (about 3 ounces) cooked chicken

2 tablespoons salsa

1 tablespoon chopped fresh cilantro

¼ cup (1 ounce) shredded Monterey Jack cheese

2 teaspoons butter or vegetable oil (optional)

1. Place 1 tortilla in large nonstick skillet; cover tortilla with spinach leaves, if desired. Place chicken in single layer over spinach. Spoon salsa over chicken. Sprinkle with cilantro; top with cheese. Place remaining tortilla on top, pressing tortilla down so filling becomes compact.

2. Cook over medium heat 4 to 5 minutes or until bottom tortilla is lightly browned. Holding top tortilla in place, gently turn over. Continue cooking 4 minutes or until bottom tortilla is browned and cheese is melted.

3. For a crispy golden finish if desired, place butter in skillet to melt; lift quesadilla to let butter flow to center of skillet. Cook 30 seconds. Turn over; continue cooking 30 seconds. Cut in half to serve.

CHICKEN BACON QUESADILLAS

MAKES 4 SERVINGS

- 4 teaspoons vegetable oil, divided
- 4 (8-inch) flour tortillas
- 1 cup (4 ounces) shredded Colby-Jack cheese
- 2 cups coarsely chopped cooked chicken
- 4 slices bacon, crisp-cooked and coarsely chopped
- ½ cup pico de gallo, plus additional for serving

  Sour cream and guacamole (optional)

1. Heat large nonstick skillet over medium heat; brush with 1 teaspoon oil. Place one tortilla in skillet; sprinkle with ¼ cup cheese. Spread ½ cup chicken over one half of tortilla; top with one fourth of bacon and 2 tablespoons pico de gallo.

2. Cook 1 to 2 minutes or until cheese is melted and bottom of tortilla is lightly browned. Fold tortilla over filling, pressing with spatula. Transfer to cutting board; cool slightly. Cut into wedges. Repeat with remaining ingredients. Serve with additional pico de gallo, sour cream and guacamole, if desired.

CAPRESE PIZZA

MAKES 6 SERVINGS

1 loaf (16 ounces) frozen pizza or bread dough, thawed

1 container (12 ounces) bruschetta sauce

1 container (8 ounces) pearl-size fresh mozzarella cheese (perlini), drained*

If pearl-size mozzarella is not available, use one (8-ounce) ball of fresh mozzarella and chop into ¼-inch pieces.

1. Preheat oven to 400°F. Spray large baking sheet with nonstick cooking spray.

2. Roll out dough on lightly floured surface into 15×10-inch rectangle. Transfer to prepared baking sheet. Cover loosely with plastic wrap; let rest 10 minutes. Meanwhile, place bruschetta sauce in colander; let drain 10 minutes.

3. Prick surface of dough several times with fork. Bake 10 minutes. Sprinkle with drained bruschetta sauce and top with mozzarella. Bake 10 minutes or until cheese is melted and crust is golden brown. Serve warm.

NOTE Bruschetta sauce is a mixture of diced fresh tomatoes, garlic, basil and olive oil. It is typically found in the refrigerated section of the supermarket with other prepared dips such as hummus.

FRIDGE-RAID Sandwiches

WHEN A CRAVING HITS, NOTHING IS BETTER THAN A QUICK AND DELICIOUS SANDWICH. YOU PROBABLY ALREADY HAVE EVERYTHING YOU NEED TO MAKE MOST OF THESE, AND IF YOU DON'T, HEAD TO THE STORE TO STOCK UP!

SOUTHWESTERN BLT

MAKES 2 SERVINGS

6 slices thick-cut applewood smoked bacon

¼ cup mayonnaise

1 teaspoon lime juice

¼ teaspoon ground chipotle pepper

¼ teaspoon ground cumin

2 pretzel rolls, split and toasted

½ cup shredded lettuce

1 large ripe tomato, cut into 4 slices

1. Cook bacon in large skillet over medium heat; drain on paper towel-lined plate.

2. Combine mayonnaise, lime juice, chipotle pepper and cumin in small bowl; mix well.

3. Spread cut sides of rolls with mayonnaise mixture. Top bottom halves of rolls with lettuce, tomato, bacon and top halves of rolls.

TUNA SALAD SANDWICH

Makes 2 servings

1 can (12 ounces) solid white albacore tuna, drained

1 can (5 ounces) chunk white albacore tuna, drained

¼ cup mayonnaise

1 tablespoon pickle relish

2 teaspoons spicy brown mustard

1 teaspoon lemon juice

½ teaspoon salt

¼ teaspoon black pepper

2 pieces focaccia (about 4×3 inches), split and toasted *or* 4 slices honey wheat bread

Lettuce, tomato and red onion slices

1. Place tuna in medium bowl; flake with fork. Add mayonnaise, relish, mustard, lemon juice, salt and pepper; mix well.

2. Serve tuna salad on focaccia with lettuce, tomato and red onion.

HOT DOG SLOPPY JOES

MAKES 2 SANDWICHES

3 to 4 hot dogs

1 tablespoon vegetable oil

2 tablespoons barbecue sauce

2 hamburger, hot dog or pretzel buns, split and toasted

1. Cut each hot dog lengthwise into ¼-inch strips (8 to 10 strips per hot dog).

2. Heat oil in large skillet over medium-high heat. Add hot dog strips; cook 5 to 7 minutes or until hot dog strips curl and are lightly browned. Add barbecue sauce; cook and stir 1 minute.

3. Pile hot dog strips in buns. Serve immediately.

 **NOTE** You can also cut the hot dogs into coin slices or quarter them lengthwise and then slice crosswise. And to make them less sloppy, try serving them in hot dog buns instead of hamburger buns.

SPEEDY MEATBALL SUBS

Makes 6 servings

1 jar (24 ounces) pasta sauce

1 pound frozen cooked Italian-style meatballs

6 sub or hoagie rolls, split

12 slices provolone cheese

Chopped fresh parsley (optional)

1. Combine pasta sauce and meatballs in large saucepan. Bring to a boil over medium heat. Reduce heat to low; cover and simmer 20 minutes or until meatballs are heated through.

2. Preheat oven to 400°F. Line baking sheet with foil. Place rolls on prepared baking sheet. Bake 3 minutes or until lightly toasted.

3. Spoon sauce and meatballs on bottom halves of rolls; top with cheese slices (two per sandwich). Bake about 3 minutes or until cheese melts. Sprinkle with parsley, if desired; top with top halves of rolls.

CHICKEN PESTO FLATBREADS

Makes 2 servings

2 tablespoons pesto

2 (6- to 7-inch) round flatbreads or Greek-style pita bread rounds (not regular pita bread or pocket bread)

1 cup packaged grilled chicken strips

4 slices mozzarella cheese

1 plum tomato, cut into ¼-inch slices

3 tablespoons shredded Parmesan cheese

1. Spread 1 tablespoon pesto over half of each flatbread. Place chicken on opposite half of bread; top with mozzarella, tomato and Parmesan. Fold pesto-topped bread half over filling.

2. Spray grill pan or nonstick skillet with nonstick cooking spray or brush with vegetable oil; heat over medium-high heat. Cook sandwiches about 3 minutes per side until bread is toasted, cheese begins to melt and sandwiches are heated through.

MAPLE FRANCHEEZIES

Makes 4 servings

MUSTARD SPREAD

- ½ cup yellow mustard
- 1 tablespoon finely chopped onion
- 1 tablespoon diced tomato
- 1 tablespoon chopped fresh parsley
- 1 teaspoon garlic powder
- ½ teaspoon black pepper

FRANCHEEZIES

- ¼ cup maple syrup
- 2 teaspoons garlic powder
- 1 teaspoon black pepper
- ½ teaspoon ground nutmeg
- 4 slices bacon
- 4 jumbo hot dogs
- 4 hot dog buns, split
- ½ cup (2 ounces) shredded Cheddar cheese

1. For mustard spread, combine mustard, onion, tomato, parsley, 1 teaspoon garlic powder and ½ teaspoon pepper in small bowl.

2. Preheat oven to 350°F.

3. Combine maple syrup, 2 teaspoons garlic powder, 1 teaspoon pepper and nutmeg in small bowl. Brush syrup mixture onto bacon slices. Wrap 1 slice bacon around each hot dog.

4. Brush hot dogs with remaining syrup mixture. Place on foil-lined baking sheet. Bake 8 to 10 minutes or until bacon is crisp and hot dogs are heated through, turning once. Place hot dogs in buns; top with mustard spread and cheese.

SUPER MEATBALL SLIDERS

MAKES 24 SLIDERS

1 can (15 ounces) whole berry cranberry sauce

1 can (about 15 ounces) tomato sauce

⅛ teaspoon red pepper flakes (optional)

2 pounds ground beef or turkey

¾ cup plain dry bread crumbs

1 egg, lightly beaten

1 package (1 ounce) dry onion soup mix

Baby arugula leaves (optional)

24 small potato rolls or dinner rolls, split

6 slices (1 ounce each) provolone cheese, cut into quarters

1. Preheat oven to 350°F. Combine cranberry sauce, tomato sauce and red pepper flakes, if desired, in medium bowl.

2. Combine beef, bread crumbs, egg and soup mix in large bowl; mix well. Shape mixture into 24 meatballs (about 1¾ inches). Place in 13×9-inch baking pan or glass baking dish; pour sauce over meatballs, making sure all meatballs are covered in sauce.

3. Bake 40 to 45 minutes or until meatballs are cooked through (160°F), basting with sauce once or twice during cooking.

4. Place arugula leaves on rolls, if desired; top with meatballs and cheese. Spoon sauce from pan over meatballs.

NOTE The meatballs can be made ahead of time. Shape them and place in the pan as directed in step 2. Cover the pan with plastic wrap. Pour the sauce over the meatballs just before baking.

BAVARIAN PRETZEL SANDWICHES

MAKES 4 SANDWICHES

4 frozen soft pretzels, thawed

1 tablespoon German mustard

2 teaspoons mayonnaise

8 slices Black Forest ham

4 slices Gouda cheese

1 tablespoon water

Coarse pretzel salt

1. Preheat oven to 350°F. Line baking sheet with parchment paper.

2. Carefully slice each pretzel in half crosswise using serrated knife. Combine mustard and mayonnaise in small bowl. Spread mustard mixture onto bottom halves of pretzels. Top with 2 slices ham, 1 slice cheese and top halves of pretzels.

3. Place sandwiches on prepared baking sheet. Brush tops of sandwiches with water; sprinkle with salt. Bake 8 minutes or until cheese is melted and pretzels are heated through.

NOTE For cold sandwiches, bake the pretzels according to package directions. When they are cool enough to handle, slice them and top with the sandwich fillings.

THANKSGIVING-ISH TURKEY SANDWICHES

Makes 4 servings

¼ cup cream cheese

¼ cup cranberry sauce or chutney

2 tablespoons chopped toasted* walnuts

8 slices multigrain or whole wheat bread, lightly toasted

½ pound sliced deli smoked turkey breast

1 cup packed mesclun or spring salad mixed greens *or* 4 red leaf lettuce leaves

*To toast walnuts, spread in single layer in small skillet. Heat over medium-low heat 2 to 3 minutes or until lightly toasted, stirring frequently.

1. Combine cream cheese and cranberry sauce in small bowl; mix well. Stir in walnuts.

2. Spread mixture on toast slices. Layer turkey and greens on 4 slices; top with remaining slices. Cut in half diagonally.

QUICK GREEK PITAS

Makes 6 servings

1 pound ground beef

1 package (10 ounces) frozen chopped spinach, thawed and well drained

4 green onions, chopped

1 can (2¼ ounces) sliced pitted black olives, drained

1 teaspoon dried oregano, divided

½ teaspoon salt

¼ teaspoon black pepper

1 large tomato, diced

1 cup plain yogurt

½ cup mayonnaise

6 (6-inch) pita breads, warmed

Lettuce leaves

1 cup (4 ounces) crumbled feta cheese

1. Brown beef in large skillet over medium-high heat 6 to 8 minutes, stirring to break up meat. Drain fat. Add spinach, green onions, olives, ½ teaspoon oregano, salt and pepper; cook and stir 2 minutes. Stir in tomato.

2. Combine yogurt, mayonnaise and remaining ½ teaspoon oregano in small bowl.

3. Cut pita in half crosswise; line inside of each pita half with lettuce. Stir cheese into beef mixture and divide among pitas. Serve with yogurt sauce.

CHERRY AND CHEESE PANINI

Makes 4 servings

1 tablespoon olive oil

1 large red onion, thinly sliced

¼ teaspoon dried thyme

2 teaspoons balsamic vinegar

⅛ teaspoon salt

⅛ teaspoon black pepper

½ cup fresh sweet cherries, pitted and chopped

4 ounces blue cheese, at room temperature

3 ounces cream cheese, softened

8 large thin slices Italian or country-style bread

1 to 2 tablespoons butter

1. Heat oil in large heavy skillet. Add onion and thyme; cook and stir over medium heat 3 minutes or until onion is tender. Stir in vinegar, salt and pepper, scraping up any browned bits from bottom of skillet. Transfer onion mixture to medium bowl; stir in cherries.

2. Mash blue cheese and cream cheese in small bowl until blended. Spread evenly over 4 bread slices. Top each slice with one fourth of cherry mixture (about ⅓ cup). Top with remaining bread slices.

3. Wipe out skillet. Melt 1 tablespoon butter in skillet. Add two sandwiches. Press down with spatula. Cook over medium heat 3 to 4 minutes per side or until golden. Repeat with remaining sandwiches, adding more butter if necessary.

STUFFED FOCACCIA SANDWICH

MAKES 4 SANDWICHES

1 container (about 5 ounces) soft cheese with garlic and herbs

1 (10-inch) round herb or onion focaccia, cut in half horizontally

½ cup thinly sliced red onion

½ cup coarsely chopped pimiento-stuffed green olives, drained

¼ cup sliced mild banana peppers

4 ounces thinly sliced deli hard salami

6 ounces thinly sliced oven-roasted turkey breast

1 package (⅔ ounce) fresh basil, stems removed

1. Spread soft cheese over cut sides of focaccia. Layer bottom half evenly with remaining ingredients. Cover sandwich with top half of focaccia; press down firmly.

2. Cut sandwich into four equal pieces. Serve immediately or wrap individually in plastic wrap and refrigerate until serving time.

"BACON" AND AVOCADO SANDWICHES

MAKES 4 SERVINGS

12 slices vegetarian bacon

½ ripe avocado

2 tablespoons mayonnaise or sour cream

1 teaspoon fresh lemon juice

8 thin slices whole wheat sandwich bread, toasted

8 slices tomato

1 cup alfalfa sprouts

1. Cook bacon according to package directions.

2. Combine avocado, mayonnaise and lemon juice in small bowl; stir with fork until smooth. Spread about 1 tablespoon avocado mixture on one side of 4 bread slices.

3. Top each with 3 slices bacon, 2 slices tomato, ¼ cup alfalfa sprouts and remaining bread slice.

NOTE   You can also make this sandwich with real bacon. For the easiest possible sandwich, use a package of pre-cooked bacon.

GRILLED THREE-CHEESE SANDWICHES

MAKES 2 SANDWICHES

2 slices (1 ounce each) Muenster cheese

2 slices (1 ounce each) Swiss cheese

2 slices (1 ounce each) Cheddar cheese

4 slices sourdough bread

2 teaspoons Dijon mustard or Dijon mustard mayonnaise

2 teaspoons butter

1. Place 1 slice of each cheese on 2 bread slices. Spread mustard over cheese; top with remaining bread slices.

2. Heat butter in large skillet over medium heat until melted. Add sandwiches; press down lightly with spatula or weigh down with small plate. Cook 4 minutes per side or until cheese is melted and sandwiches are golden brown.

PARTY Munchies

WHEN IT'S TIME FOR SOCIAL SNACKING, PUT IN THE EXTRA EFFORT AND MAKE SOME IMPRESSIVELY DELICIOUS MUNCHIES.

JALAPEÑO POPPERS

MAKES 20 TO 24 POPPERS

10 to 12 fresh jalapeño peppers*

1 package (8 ounces) cream cheese, softened

1½ cups (6 ounces) shredded Cheddar cheese, divided

2 green onions, finely chopped

½ teaspoon onion powder

¼ teaspoon salt

⅛ teaspoon garlic powder

6 slices bacon, crisp-cooked and finely chopped

2 tablespoons grated Parmesan or Romano cheese

For large jalapeño peppers, use 10. For small peppers, use 12.

1. Preheat oven to 375°F. Line baking sheet with parchment paper or foil.

2. Cut each jalapeño in half lengthwise; remove ribs and seeds.

3. Combine cream cheese, 1 cup Cheddar cheese, green onions, onion powder, salt and garlic powder in medium bowl. Stir in bacon. Fill each jalapeño half with about 1 tablespoon cheese mixture. Place on prepared baking sheet. Sprinkle with remaining ½ cup Cheddar cheese and Parmesan cheese.

4. Bake 10 to 12 minutes or until cheese is melted and jalapeños are slightly softened.

PEPPERONI BREAD

MAKES ABOUT 6 SERVINGS

1 package (about 14 ounces) refrigerated pizza dough

8 slices provolone cheese

20 to 30 slices pepperoni (about half of 6-ounce package)

½ teaspoon Italian seasoning

¾ cup (3 ounces) shredded mozzarella cheese

½ cup grated Parmesan cheese

1 egg, beaten

Marinara sauce, heated

1. Preheat oven to 400°F. Unroll pizza dough on sheet of parchment paper with long side in front of you. Cut off corners of dough to create oval shape.

2. Arrange half of provolone slices over bottom half of oval, cutting to fit as necessary. Top with pepperoni; sprinkle with ¼ teaspoon Italian seasoning. Top with mozzarella, Parmesan and remaining provolone slices; sprinkle with remaining ¼ teaspoon Italian seasoning.

3. Fold top half of dough over filling to create half moon (calzone) shape; press edges with fork or pinch edges to seal. Transfer calzone with parchment paper to large baking sheet; curve slightly into crescent shape. Brush with beaten egg.

4. Bake about 16 minutes or until crust is golden brown. Remove to wire rack to cool slightly. Cut crosswise into slices; serve warm with marinara sauce.

TEX-MEX NACHOS

Makes 4 to 6 servings

1 tablespoon vegetable oil

8 ounces ground beef

½ cup chopped onion

2 cloves garlic, minced

2 teaspoons chili powder

1 teaspoon ground cumin

½ teaspoon salt

½ teaspoon dried oregano

1 can (about 15 ounces) kidney beans, rinsed and drained

½ cup corn

½ cup sour cream, divided

2 tablespoons mayonnaise

1 tablespoon lime juice

¼ to ½ teaspoon chipotle chili powder

½ bag tortilla chips

½ (15-ounce) jar Cheddar cheese dip, warmed

½ cup pico de gallo

¼ cup guacamole

1 cup shredded iceberg lettuce

2 jalapeño peppers, thinly sliced into rings

1. Heat oil in large skillet over medium-high heat. Add beef, onion and garlic; cook and stir 6 to 8 minutes or until beef is no longer pink. Add chili powder, cumin, salt and oregano; cook and stir 1 minute. Add beans and corn; reduce heat to medium-low and cook 3 minutes or until heated through.

2. For chipotle sauce, combine ¼ cup sour cream, mayonnaise, lime juice and chipotle chili powder in small bowl; mix well. Place in small plastic squeeze bottle.

3. Spread tortilla chips on platter or large plate. Top with beef mixture; drizzle with cheese dip. Top with pico de gallo, guacamole, remaining ¼ cup sour cream, lettuce and jalapeños. Squeeze chipotle sauce over nachos. Serve immediately.

CREAMY CRAB DIP
MAKES 6 TO 8 SERVINGS (ABOUT 3½ CUPS)

½ (8-ounce) package cream cheese, softened

½ cup sour cream

2 tablespoons mayonnaise

¾ teaspoon seasoned salt

¼ teaspoon paprika, plus additional for garnish

2 cans (6 ounces each) crabmeat, drained and flaked

½ cup (2 ounces) shredded mozzarella cheese

2 tablespoons minced onion

2 tablespoons finely chopped green bell pepper*

Chopped fresh parsley (optional)

Tortilla chips

*For a spicier dip, substitute 1 tablespoon minced jalapeño pepper for the bell pepper.

1. Preheat oven to 350°F.

2. Combine cream cheese, sour cream, mayonnaise, seasoned salt and ¼ teaspoon paprika in medium bowl; stir until well blended and smooth. Add crabmeat, cheese, onion and bell pepper; stir until blended. Spread in small (1-quart) shallow baking dish.

3. Bake 15 to 20 minutes or until bubbly and top is beginning to brown. Garnish with additional paprika and parsley; serve with tortilla chips.

SPINACH FLORENTINE FLATBREAD

MAKES 8 SERVINGS

1 tablespoon olive oil

2 cloves garlic, minced

1 package (10 ounces) baby spinach

1 can (about 14 ounces) quartered artichokes, drained and sliced

½ teaspoon salt

¼ teaspoon dried oregano

Black pepper

Red pepper flakes

2 rectangular pizza or flatbread crusts (about 8 ounces each)*

1 plum tomato, seeded and diced

2 cups (8 ounces) shredded Monterey Jack cheese

½ cup (2 ounces) shredded Italian cheese blend

Shredded fresh basil leaves (optional)

Look for packaged flatbreads in the bakery section of the grocery store.

1. Preheat oven to 425°F.

2. Heat oil in large nonstick skillet over medium-high heat. Add garlic; cook and stir 30 seconds. Add half of spinach; cook and stir until slightly wilted. Add additional spinach by handfuls; cook about 3 minutes or until completely wilted, stirring occasionally. Transfer to medium bowl; stir in artichokes, salt and oregano. Season with black pepper and red pepper flakes.

3. Place pizza crusts on large baking sheet. Spread spinach mixture over crusts; sprinkle with tomato, Monterey Jack cheese and Italian cheese blend.

4. Bake 12 minutes or until cheeses are melted and edges of crusts are browned. Garnish with basil.

 **TIP** For crispier crusts, bake flatbreads on a preheated pizza stone or directly on the oven rack.

PRETZEL STICKS WITH BEER-CHEESE DIP

Makes 6 to 8 servings (2 cups dip)

PRETZELS

- 1⅔ cups warm water (110°F)
- 1 package (¼ ounce) active dry yeast
- 2 teaspoons sugar
- 1 teaspoon table salt
- 4½ cups all-purpose flour
- 2 tablespoons butter, softened
- 2 tablespoons vegetable oil
- 12 cups water
- ½ cup baking soda
- Kosher salt or pretzel salt and sesame seeds

HONEY-MUSTARD DIP

- ⅓ cup sour cream
- ¼ cup Dijon mustard
- 3 tablespoons honey

BEER-CHEESE DIP

- 2 tablespoons butter
- 1 clove garlic, minced
- 2 tablespoons all-purpose flour
- 1 tablespoon Dijon mustard
- 1 teaspoon Worcestershire sauce
- 1 cup Belgian white ale
- 2 cups (8 ounces) shredded white Cheddar cheese
- 1 cup (4 ounces) shredded Monterey Jack cheese
- Black pepper (optional)

1. For pretzels, combine 1⅔ cups warm water, yeast, sugar and 1 teaspoon salt in large bowl of electric stand mixer; stir to dissolve yeast. Let stand 5 minutes or until bubbly. Add 4½ cups flour and softened butter; beat at low speed until combined, scraping side of bowl occasionally. Replace paddle attachment with dough hook; knead at medium-low speed 5 minutes.

2. Place dough in large greased bowl; turn to coat top. Cover and let rise in warm place 1 hour or until doubled in size.

3. For mustard dip, combine sour cream, ¼ cup mustard and honey in small bowl; mix well. Refrigerate until ready to use.

4. Preheat oven to 450°F. Brush 1 tablespoon oil over each of two large baking sheets. Bring 12 cups water to a boil in large saucepan or Dutch oven.

5. Punch down dough; turn out onto floured work surface. Cut into 14 equal pieces. Roll each piece into 12-inch-long rope. Cut each rope in half.

6. Carefully stir baking soda into boiling water. Working in batches, drop dough pieces into boiling water; cook 30 seconds. Remove to prepared baking sheets with slotted spoon. Make 3 to 4 slashes in each pretzel stick with sharp knife. Sprinkle with kosher salt and sesame seeds.

7. Bake 14 to 15 minutes or until dark golden brown, rotating baking sheets halfway through baking time. Cool slightly on wire rack.

8. Meanwhile for cheese dip, melt 2 tablespoons butter in medium saucepan over medium heat. Add garlic; cook and stir 1 minute. Whisk in 2 tablespoons flour until well blended; cook 1 minute. Whisk in 1 tablespoon mustard and Worcestershire sauce. Slowly whisk in ale in thin steady stream. Cook 1 minute or until slightly thickened. Add cheeses by $\frac{1}{4}$ cupfuls, stirring until cheeses are melted before adding next addition. Transfer to serving bowl; sprinkle with pepper, if desired. Serve pretzels warm with dips.

 **TIP** If making pretzels seems like too much work, buy pretzel rolls (either round or oblong/sausage shape) instead. Heat them in the oven just until warm, tear them into bite-size pieces or slice them crosswise and serve them with the dips.

CHEESY GARLIC BREAD

MAKES 8 TO 10 SERVINGS

1 loaf (about 16 ounces) Italian bread

½ cup (1 stick) butter, softened

8 cloves garlic, very thinly sliced

¼ cup grated Parmesan cheese

2 cups (8 ounces) shredded mozzarella cheese

1. Preheat oven to 425°F. Line large baking sheet with foil.

2. Cut bread in half horizontally. Spread cut sides of bread evenly with butter; top with sliced garlic. Sprinkle with Parmesan, then mozzarella. Place on prepared baking sheet.

3. Bake 12 minutes or until cheeses are melted and golden brown in spots. Cut crosswise into slices. Serve warm.

SWEET SOY GINGER CHICKEN

Makes 4 to 6 servings

SAUCE

- ¾ cup water
- 1 tablespoon cornstarch
- ¼ cup packed dark brown sugar
- ¼ cup soy sauce
- 3 tablespoons lime juice
- 2 tablespoons minced fresh ginger
- 1 teaspoon minced garlic
- ¼ teaspoon red pepper flakes

CHICKEN

- 2 large boneless skinless chicken breasts (about 2 pounds)
- 1 cup all-purpose flour
- ¼ cup cornstarch
- 2 teaspoons salt
- ¼ teaspoon black pepper
- ¼ teaspoon ground red pepper
- ¼ teaspoon paprika
- 2 eggs
- ½ cup milk
  Vegetable oil for frying
  Ranch dressing (optional)

1. For sauce, whisk water and cornstarch in medium saucepan until smooth. Add brown sugar, soy sauce, lime juice, ginger, garlic and red pepper flakes; whisk until well blended. Bring to a boil over high heat. Reduce heat to low; simmer 10 minutes or until thickened, stirring occasionally. Transfer to large bowl; set aside to cool.

2. Cut chicken into large pieces (about 2×1 inches). Combine flour, cornstarch, salt, black pepper, ground red pepper and paprika in large bowl. Whisk eggs and milk in shallow bowl. Coat chicken with flour mixture. Dip in egg mixture, letting excess drip back into bowl. Coat again with flour mixture; place on baking sheet.

3. Heat 3 inches of oil in large saucepan over medium-high heat to 375°F; adjust heat to maintain temperature during frying. Cook chicken in batches 3 minutes or until golden brown and cooked through, turning once. Drain on paper towel-lined plate. Add chicken to sauce and stir to coat. Remove to serving plate with slotted spoon. Serve with ranch dressing, if desired.

TOASTED RAVIOLI
MAKES 20 TO 24 RAVIOLI

1 cup all-purpose flour

2 eggs

¼ cup water

1 cup plain dry bread crumbs

1 teaspoon Italian seasoning

¾ teaspoon garlic powder

¼ teaspoon salt

½ cup grated Parmesan cheese

2 tablespoons finely chopped fresh parsley

1 package (12 to 16 ounces) meat or cheese ravioli, thawed if frozen

Vegetable oil for frying

Pasta sauce, heated

1. Place flour in shallow bowl. Whisk eggs and water in another shallow bowl. Combine bread crumbs, Italian seasoning, garlic powder and salt in third shallow bowl. Combine cheese and parsley in large bowl; stir to blend.

2. Coat ravioli with flour. Dip in egg mixture, letting excess drip back into bowl. Roll in bread crumb mixture to coat.

3. Heat 2 inches of oil in large deep skillet over medium-high heat to 350°F; adjust heat to maintain temperature during frying. Working in batches, carefully add ravioli to hot oil; cook 1 minute or until golden brown, turning once. Remove from oil with slotted spoon; drain on paper towel-lined plate. Add to bowl with cheese; toss to coat. Serve warm with pasta sauce.

GREEN BEAN FRIES

MAKES 4 TO 6 SERVINGS

8 ounces fresh green beans, trimmed

½ cup all-purpose flour

½ cup cornstarch

¾ cup milk

1 egg

1 cup plain dry bread crumbs

1 teaspoon salt

½ teaspoon onion powder

¼ teaspoon garlic powder

Vegetable oil for frying

Ranch dressing or garlic aïoli

1. Bring large saucepan of salted water to a boil. Add green beans; cook 4 minutes or until crisp-tender. Drain and run under cold running water to stop cooking.

2. Combine flour and cornstarch in large bowl. Whisk milk and egg in another large bowl. Combine bread crumbs, salt, onion powder and garlic powder in shallow bowl. Place green beans in flour mixture; toss to coat. Working in batches, coat beans with egg mixture, letting excess drain back into bowl. Roll beans in bread crumb mixture to coat. Place on large baking sheet.

3. Heat 3 inches of oil in large saucepan over medium-high heat to 375°F; adjust heat to maintain temperature during frying. Cook green beans in batches about 1 minute or until golden brown; adjust heat to maintain temperature. Drain on paper towel-lined plate. Serve warm with ranch dressing.

BUFFALO WINGS

MAKES 4 SERVINGS

1 cup hot pepper sauce

⅓ cup vegetable oil, plus additional for frying

1 teaspoon sugar

½ teaspoon ground red pepper

½ teaspoon garlic powder

½ teaspoon Worcestershire sauce

⅛ teaspoon black pepper

1 pound chicken wings, tips discarded, separated at joints

Blue cheese or ranch dressing

Celery sticks

1. Combine hot pepper sauce, ⅓ cup oil, sugar, red pepper, garlic powder, Worcestershire sauce and black pepper in small saucepan; cook over medium heat 20 minutes. Pour sauce into large bowl.

2. Heat 3 inches of oil in large saucepan over medium-high heat to 350°F; adjust heat to maintain temperature during frying. Add wings; cook 10 minutes or until crispy. Drain on wire rack set over paper towels.

3. Transfer wings to bowl of sauce; toss to coat. Serve with blue cheese dressing and celery sticks.

POTATO SKINS

MAKES 6 TO 8 SERVINGS

8 medium baking potatoes (6 to 8 ounces each), unpeeled

1 tablespoon vegetable oil

1 teaspoon salt

⅛ teaspoon black pepper

1 tablespoon butter, melted

1 cup (4 ounces) shredded Cheddar cheese

8 slices bacon, crisp-cooked and coarsely chopped

1 cup sour cream

3 tablespoons snipped fresh chives

1. Preheat oven to 400°F.

2. Prick potatoes all over with fork. Rub oil over potatoes; sprinkle with salt and pepper. Place in 13×9-inch baking pan. Bake 1 hour or until fork-tender. Let stand until cool enough to handle. *Reduce oven temperature to 350°F.*

3. Cut potatoes in half lengthwise; cut small slice off bottom of each half so potato halves lay flat. Scoop out soft middles of potato skins; reserve for another use. Place potato halves, skin sides up, in baking pan; brush potato skins with butter.

4. Bake 20 to 25 minutes or until crisp. Turn potatoes over; top with cheese and bacon. Bake 5 minutes or until cheese is melted. Cool slightly. Top with sour cream and chives just before serving.

MOZZARELLA STICKS
Makes 4 to 6 servings

¼ cup all-purpose flour

2 eggs

1 tablespoon water

1 cup plain dry bread crumbs

2 teaspoons Italian seasoning

½ teaspoon salt

½ teaspoon garlic powder

1 package (12 ounces) string cheese (12 sticks)

Vegetable oil for frying

1 cup marinara or pizza sauce, heated

1. Place flour in shallow bowl. Whisk eggs and water in another shallow bowl. Combine bread crumbs, Italian seasoning, salt and garlic powder in third shallow bowl.

2. Coat each piece of cheese with flour. Dip in egg mixture, letting excess drip back into bowl. Roll in bread crumb mixture to coat. Dip again in egg mixture and roll again in bread crumb mixture. Refrigerate until ready to cook.

3. Heat 2 inches of oil in large saucepan over medium-high heat to 350°F; adjust heat to maintain temperature during frying. Add cheese sticks; cook about 1 minute or until golden brown. Drain on wire rack. Serve with warm marinara sauce for dipping.

PEPPERONI PIZZA ROLLS

MAKES 12 ROLLS

1 loaf (16 ounces) frozen pizza dough or white bread dough, thawed according to package directions

½ cup pizza sauce, plus additional sauce for serving

⅓ cup chopped pepperoni or mini pepperoni slices (half of 2½-ounce package)

9 to 10 slices fontina, provolone or provolone-mozzarella blend cheese*

For best results, use thinner cheese slices (less than 1 ounce each).

1. Spray 12 standard (2½-inch) muffin pan cups with nonstick cooking spray.

2. Roll out dough on lightly floured surface into 12×10-inch rectangle. Spread ½ cup pizza sauce over dough, leaving ½-inch border on one long side. Sprinkle with pepperoni; top with cheese, cutting slices to fit as necessary. Starting with long side opposite ½-inch border, roll up dough tightly; pinch seam to seal.

3. Cut crosswise into 1-inch slices; place slices cut sides up in prepared muffin cups. Cover with plastic wrap; let rise in warm place 30 to 40 minutes or until nearly doubled in size. Preheat oven to 350°F.

4. Bake about 25 minutes or until golden brown. Loosen bottom and sides with small spatula or knife; remove to wire rack. Serve warm with additional sauce for dipping, if desired.

SUPER SIMPLE CHEESY BUBBLE LOAF

Makes 12 servings

2 packages (7½ ounces each) refrigerated buttermilk biscuits (10 biscuits per package)

2 tablespoons butter, melted

1½ cups (6 ounces) shredded Italian cheese blend

1. Preheat oven to 350°F. Spray 9×5-inch loaf pan with nonstick cooking spray.

2. Separate biscuits; cut each biscuit into four pieces with scissors. Layer half of biscuit pieces in prepared pan. Drizzle with 1 tablespoon butter; sprinkle with 1 cup cheese. Top with remaining biscuit pieces, 1 tablespoon butter and ½ cup cheese.

3. Bake about 25 minutes or until golden brown. Serve warm.

TIP

It's easy to change up the flavors in this simple bread. Try Mexican cheese blend instead of Italian, and add taco seasoning and/or hot pepper sauce to the melted butter before drizzling it over the dough. Or, sprinkle ¼ cup chopped ham, salami or crumbled crisp-cooked bacon between the layers of dough.

ITALIAN SUB CROSTINI
MAKES 12 CROSTINI

1 small loaf (6 inches) French bread, cut into ½-inch slices

Olive oil

1 ball (8 ounces) fresh mozzarella cheese, cut into 12 slices

8 ounces sliced prosciutto

Fresh basil leaves (optional)

1. Preheat oven to 400°F. Brush bread slices with oil. Place on ungreased baking sheet. Bake 5 minutes or until crisp.

2. Place 1 slice of mozzarella on each toast. Top each with 1 slice of prosciutto.

3. Bake 3 minutes or until cheese is melted. Garnish with basil. Serve immediately.

MORNING Munchies

WHEN THE MUNCHIES HIT IN THE MORNING, MAKE ONE OF THESE DELICIOUS BREAKFAST SNACKS WITH MINIMAL EFFORT.

BREAKFAST SAUSAGE MONKEY MUFFINS

Makes 12 muffins

12 ounces bulk pork sausage

1 egg, beaten

1½ cups (6 ounces) shredded Mexican cheese blend, divided

2 packages (7½ ounces each) refrigerated buttermilk biscuits (10 biscuits per package)

1. Preheat oven to 350°F. Spray 12 standard (2½-inch) muffin cups with nonstick cooking spray.

2. Cook and stir sausage in large skillet over medium-high heat about 8 minutes or until no longer pink, breaking apart any large pieces. Spoon sausage and drippings into large bowl; let cool 2 minutes. Add egg; stir until blended. Stir in 1¼ cups cheese.

3. Separate biscuits; cut each biscuit into 4 pieces with scissors. Roll biscuit pieces in sausage mixture to coat; place 6 to 7 biscuit pieces in each muffin cup. Sprinkle with remaining ¼ cup cheese.

4. Bake about 22 minutes or until golden brown. Remove muffins to paper towel-lined plate. Serve warm.

UPSIDE DOWN PANCAKE MUFFINS

Makes 16 muffins

2 cups buttermilk pancake mix

1½ cups water

16 teaspoons maple syrup, plus additional for serving

1 cup fresh or frozen blueberries, raspberries, blackberries or a combination (do not thaw frozen berries)

Butter

Powdered sugar (optional)

1. Preheat oven to 350°F. Spray 16 standard (2½-inch) muffin cups with nonstick cooking spray.

2. Whisk pancake mix and water in 4-cup measuring cup with spout; let stand 3 minutes. Pour batter into prepared muffin cups, filling three-fourths full. Add 1 teaspoon syrup to each cup (do not stir); top with 1 tablespoon berries.

3. Bake 15 minutes or until tops are set and toothpick inserted into centers comes out clean. Loosen bottom and sides of cups with small spatula or knife; invert onto wire rack. If some of berries stick to pan, gently scrape from pan and place on top of muffins. Serve warm with butter and additional maple syrup. Sprinkle with powdered sugar, if desired.

RAMEN FRENCH TOAST

MAKES 4 SLICES

2 eggs

½ cup milk

¼ cup maple syrup, plus additional for serving

1 teaspoon ground cinnamon

2 packages (3 ounces each) ramen noodles, any flavor*

1 tablespoon butter

Discard seasoning packets.

1. Whisk eggs, milk, ¼ cup maple syrup and cinnamon in 13×9-inch glass baking dish. Carefully break each noodle block into two square pieces of "bread." Place in egg mixture, turn to coat both sides. Let stand 30 minutes to lightly soften, turning once.

2. Heat butter in large skillet over medium heat. Add noodle pieces. Cook 3 minutes per side until golden brown.

3. Cut in half diagonally. Serve with additional syrup.

MINI SPINACH FRITTATAS
MAKES 12 MINI FRITTATAS

 1 tablespoon olive oil

 ½ cup chopped onion

 8 eggs

 ¼ cup plain yogurt

 1 package (10 ounces) frozen chopped spinach, thawed and squeezed dry

 ½ cup (2 ounces) shredded white Cheddar cheese

 ¼ cup grated Parmesan cheese

 ¾ teaspoon salt

 ⅛ teaspoon black pepper

 ⅛ teaspoon ground red pepper

    Dash ground nutmeg

1. Preheat oven to 350°F. Spray 12 standard (2½-inch) muffin cups with nonstick cooking spray.

2. Heat oil in large nonstick skillet over medium heat. Add onion; cook and stir about 5 minutes or until tender. Set aside to cool slightly.

3. Whisk eggs and yogurt in large bowl. Stir in spinach, Cheddar, Parmesan, salt, black pepper, red pepper, nutmeg and onion until blended. Divide mixture evenly among prepared muffin cups.

4. Bake 20 to 25 minutes or until eggs are puffed and firm and no longer shiny. Cool in pan 2 minutes. Loosen bottom and sides with small spatula or knife; remove to wire rack. Serve warm, cold or at room temperature.

MINI FRUIT COFFEECAKES

MAKES 12 SERVINGS

1 package (about 17 ounces) frozen puff pastry (2 sheets), thawed

1 package (8 ounces) cream cheese, softened

1 egg

2 tablespoons granulated sugar

¼ cup desired fruit filling (apricot jam, strawberry jam, lemon curd or a combination)

½ cup powdered sugar (optional)

2 teaspoons milk (optional)

1. Preheat oven to 350°F. Spray 12 standard (2½-inch) muffin cups with nonstick cooking spray.

2. Unroll puff pastry on work surface; cut each sheet into six rectangles. Fit pastry into prepared muffin cups, pressing into bottoms and up sides of cups. (Two sides of each rectangle will extend up over top of muffin pan.)

3. Beat cream cheese in large bowl with electric mixer at medium-high speed until smooth. Add egg and granulated sugar; beat until well blended. Spoon heaping tablespoon cream cheese mixture into each cup; top with 1 teaspoon filling. Snip center of each overhanging pastry with scissors or paring knife; fold resulting four flaps in over filling, overlapping slightly (as you would fold a box).

4. Bake 20 minutes or until pastry is golden and filling is set and puffed. Cool in pan 2 minutes; remove to wire rack to cool slightly.

5. Meanwhile, prepare glaze, if desired. Whisk powdered sugar and milk in small bowl until smooth. Drizzle over coffeecakes.

BREAKFAST BISCUIT BAKE

Makes 8 servings

8 ounces bacon, chopped

1 small onion, finely chopped

1 clove garlic, minced

¼ teaspoon red pepper flakes

5 eggs

¼ cup milk

½ cup (2 ounces) shredded white Cheddar cheese, divided

¼ teaspoon salt

⅛ teaspoon black pepper

1 package (16 ounces) refrigerated jumbo buttermilk biscuits (8 biscuits)

1. Preheat oven to 425°F. Cook bacon in large cast iron skillet until crisp. Remove to paper towel-lined plate. Drain off and reserve drippings, leaving 1 tablespoon in skillet.

2. Add onion, garlic and red pepper flakes to skillet; cook and stir 8 minutes or until onion is softened. Set aside to cool slightly.

3. Whisk eggs, milk, ¼ cup cheese, salt and black pepper in medium bowl until well blended. Stir in onion mixture.

4. Wipe out any onion mixture remaining in skillet; grease with additional drippings, if necessary. Separate biscuits and arrange in single layer in bottom of skillet. (Bottom of skillet should be completely covered.) Pour egg mixture over biscuits; sprinkle with remaining ¼ cup cheese and cooked bacon.

5. Bake about 25 minutes or until puffed and golden brown. Serve warm.

CHEDDAR JALAPEÑO CORNMEAL WAFFLES

Makes 8 servings

¾ cup all-purpose flour

1¼ cups medium-grind yellow cornmeal

2 tablespoons sugar

2 teaspoons baking powder

½ teaspoon baking soda

1 teaspoon salt

¾ cup (3 ounces) shredded sharp Cheddar cheese

1 jalapeño pepper, sliced into thin rings

2 eggs

2 cups buttermilk

6 tablespoons butter, melted and slightly cooled

1. Preheat oven to 200°F. Preheat classic waffle maker to medium-high heat. Set wire rack on large baking sheet.

2. Whisk flour, cornmeal, sugar, baking powder, baking soda and salt in large bowl until combined. Stir in cheese and jalapeño.

3. Whisk eggs in medium bowl. Whisk in buttermilk and butter until well blended. Add to flour mixture; stir until combined.

4. Pour ½ cup batter into center of waffle maker; close lid and cook 3 to 5 minutes or until golden brown and crisp. Remove to wire rack; keep warm in oven. Repeat with remaining batter.

 **TIP** Save some leftovers for lunch or dinner, and serve reheated with chili.

QUICK BREAKFAST SANDWICH

Makes 2 sandwiches

2 breakfast sausage patties

3 eggs

Salt and black pepper

2 teaspoons butter

2 slices (about 2 ounces) Cheddar cheese

2 whole wheat English muffins, split and toasted

1. Cook sausage according to package directions; keep warm.

2. Beat eggs, salt and pepper in small bowl. Melt butter in small skillet over low heat. Pour eggs into skillet; cook and stir just until set.

3. Place cheese on bottom halves of English muffins; top with sausage and scrambled eggs. Serve immediately.

CARAMELIZED BACON

MAKES 6 SERVINGS

12 slices (about 12 ounces) applewood-smoked bacon

½ cup packed brown sugar

2 tablespoons water

¼ to ½ teaspoon ground red pepper

1. Preheat oven to 375°F. Line large rimmed baking sheet with foil. Spray wire rack with nonstick cooking spray; place on baking sheet.

2. Cut bacon in half crosswise, if desired; arrange in single layer on prepared wire rack. Combine brown sugar, water and ground red pepper in small bowl; mix well. Brush generously over bacon.

3. Bake 20 to 25 minutes or until bacon is well browned. Immediately remove to serving platter; cool completely.

 Bacon can be prepared up to 3 days ahead and stored in the refrigerator between sheets of waxed paper in a resealable food storage bag. Let stand at room temperature at least 30 minutes before serving.

BREAKFAST QUESADILLAS

Makes 4 servings

4 eggs

2 tablespoons milk

¼ teaspoon salt

⅛ teaspoon black pepper

4 teaspoons canola oil, divided

1 can (4 ounces) chopped mild green chiles

8 soft corn tortillas

½ cup (2 ounces) shredded sharp Cheddar cheese

¼ cup chopped fresh cilantro

1 ounce pepperoni slices, quartered

1. Whisk eggs, milk, salt and pepper in small bowl. Heat 2 teaspoons oil in large skillet over medium heat. Cook eggs until set, lifting edges to allow uncooked portion to flow underneath. Remove from skillet. Wipe out skillet with paper towel.

2. Spread 1 tablespoon chiles on half of each tortilla. Top each with eggs, cheese and cilantro; sprinkle evenly with pepperoni. Fold tortillas in half.

3. Heat remaining 2 teaspoons oil in skillet. Cook quesadillas in two batches 3 minutes per side or until cheese is melted.

POUND CAKE DIP STICKS

MAKES 8 TO 10 SERVINGS

½ cup raspberry jam, divided

1 package (10¾ ounces) frozen pound cake

1½ cups cold whipping cream

1. Preheat oven to 400°F. Spray baking sheet with nonstick cooking spray. Microwave ¼ cup jam on HIGH 30 seconds or until smooth.

2. Cut pound cake into 10 (½-inch) slices. Brush one side of slices lightly with warm jam. Cut each slice lengthwise into 3 sticks. Place sticks, jam side up, on prepared baking sheet.

3. Bake 10 minutes or until cake sticks are crisp and light golden brown. Remove to wire rack.

4. Meanwhile, whip cream in large bowl with electric mixer, hand mixer or whisk until soft peaks form. Add remaining ¼ cup raspberry jam; whip until combined. Serve with cake sticks.

FRUITED WAFFLE PARFAIT CUP

MAKES 4 SERVINGS

1 prepared frozen or leftover Belgian waffle, torn into bite-size pieces

½ cup raspberry jam

½ teaspoon almond extract

1 cup plain or vanilla yogurt

2 cups chopped fresh peaches or thawed frozen peaches

1. Place equal amounts of waffle pieces in each of four parfait dishes.

2. Place jam in small microwavable bowl; microwave on HIGH 30 seconds to slightly melt. Stir in almond extract until smooth. Spoon over waffle pieces; top with yogurt and fruit.

MEXICAN BREAKFAST BURRITO

Makes 4 servings

8 eggs

2 teaspoons butter

⅓ cup canned black beans, rinsed and drained

2 tablespoons sliced green onions

½ teaspoon salt

⅛ teaspoon black pepper

2 (10-inch) flour tortillas

¼ cup (1 ounce) shredded Cheddar cheese

3 tablespoons salsa

1. Whisk eggs in medium bowl until well blended. Melt butter in large nonstick skillet over medium heat. Pour in eggs; cook 5 to 7 minutes or until mixture begins to set, stirring occasionally. Stir in beans, green onions, salt and pepper; cook and stir 3 minutes or just until cooked through.

2. Spoon mixture evenly down centers of tortillas; top evenly with cheese. Roll up to enclose filling. Cut in half; serve with salsa.

WITH JUST A FEW INGREDIENTS AND A LITTLE BIT OF PREP, YOU'RE MINUTES AWAY FROM CRAVABLE SWEET SNACKS THAT ARE IMPOSSIBLE TO PUT DOWN.

PEANUTTY BANANA-RAMA TREATS

MAKES 24 SERVINGS

¼ cup (½ stick) butter

1 cup crunchy peanut butter

1 bag (10 ounces) mini marshmallows

1 package (3.4 ounces) banana cream instant pudding mix

5 packages (3 ounces each) ramen noodles, any flavor, crushed into small pieces*

Discard seasoning packets.

1. Spray 9-inch square baking pan with nonstick cooking spray.

2. Melt butter in large saucepan over medium heat. Stir in peanut butter and marshmallows, stirring constantly until completely melted. Remove from heat; fold in pudding mix until fully combined. Fold in noodles.

3. Immediately pour into prepared pan. Using buttered fingers, gently press mixture into pan. Let stand at least 30 minutes before cutting.

BANANA SPLIT DUMP CAKE

Makes 12 to 16 servings

1 can (20 ounces) crushed pineapple, undrained

1 can (14½ ounces) tart cherries in water, drained

1 package (about 18 ounces) banana cake mix

½ cup (1 stick) butter, cut into thin slices

½ cup semisweet chocolate chips

½ cup chopped pecans

Whipped cream and maraschino cherries (optional)

1. Preheat oven to 350°F. Spray 13×9-inch baking pan with nonstick cooking spray.

2. Spread pineapple and cherries in prepared pan. Top with cake mix, spreading evenly. Top with butter in single layer, covering cake mix as much as possible. Sprinkle with chocolate chips and pecans.

3. Bake 55 to 60 minutes or until toothpick inserted into center of cake comes out clean. Cool at least 15 minutes before serving. Top with whipped cream and cherries, if desired.

SWEET Snacks

FUDGY MARSHMALLOW POPCORN

MAKES ABOUT 4 QUARTS

3½ quarts popped popcorn (about 14 cups)

2 cups sugar

1 cup evaporated milk

¼ cup (½ stick) butter

1 cup marshmallow creme (½ of 7-ounce jar)

1 cup semisweet chocolate chips

1 teaspoon vanilla

1. Spray baking sheets with nonstick cooking spray or line with parchment paper. Place popcorn in large bowl.

2. Combine sugar, evaporated milk and butter in medium saucepan. Cook over medium heat until sugar is dissolved and mixture comes to a boil, stirring constantly.* Boil 5 minutes. Remove from heat. Stir in marshmallow creme, chocolate chips and vanilla until chocolate is melted and mixture is smooth.

3. Pour chocolate mixture over popcorn, stirring until completely coated. Spread in single layer on prepared baking sheets. Refrigerate until set.

*If sugar mixture sticks to the pan, wash down side of pan with pastry brush dipped in hot water to remove crystals.

HINT Remove any unpopped kernels before measuring the popped popcorn.

DOUBLE PINEAPPLE BERRY DUMP CAKE

MAKES 12 TO 16 SERVINGS

1 can (20 ounces) crushed pineapple, undrained

1 package (12 ounces) frozen mixed berries, thawed and drained

1 package (about 15 ounces) pineapple cake mix

½ cup (1 stick) butter, cut into thin slices

Whipped cream (optional)

1. Preheat oven to 350°F. Spray 13×9-inch baking pan with nonstick cooking spray.

2. Spread pineapple and berries in prepared pan. Top with cake mix, spreading evenly. Top with butter in single layer, covering cake mix as much as possible.

3. Bake 45 to 50 minutes or until toothpick inserted into center of cake comes out clean. Cool at least 15 minutes before serving. Serve with whipped cream, if desired.

FUGDY BROWNIES

Makes 2 to 3 dozen brownies

1 cup (2 sticks) butter

8 ounces semisweet baking chocolate, coarsely chopped

1 cup sugar

4 eggs

1 teaspoon vanilla

1 teaspoon salt

1¼ cups all-purpose flour

2 cups dark or semisweet chocolate chips, divided

¼ cup whipping cream

1 container (about 2 ounces) rainbow nonpareils

1. Preheat oven to 350°F. Spray 13×9-inch baking pan with nonstick cooking spray or line with parchment paper.

2. Heat butter and chocolate in large heavy saucepan over low heat; stir until melted and smooth. Remove from heat; stir in sugar until blended. Stir in eggs, one at a time, until well blended after each addition. Stir in vanilla and salt. Add flour and 1 cup chocolate chips; stir just until blended. Spread batter evenly in prepared pan.

3. Bake 22 to 25 minutes or until center is set and toothpick inserted into center comes out clean. Cool completely in pan on wire rack.

4. Heat cream in small saucepan over medium-low heat until bubbles appear around edge of pan. Remove from heat; add remaining 1 cup chocolate chips. Let stand 1 minute; whisk until smooth and well blended. Spread evenly over brownies; top with nonpareils.

LEFTOVER CANDY BARK

MAKES ABOUT 3 POUNDS

3 cups chopped leftover
   chocolate candy

2 packages (12 ounces each)
   white chocolate chips

1 package (10 ounces)
   peanut butter chips

1. Line 13×9-inch baking pan with parchment paper. Spread candy in prepared baking pan and freeze at least 1 hour.

2. Melt white chocolate and peanut butter chips in large microwavable bowl on HIGH at 45-second intervals, stirring after each interval, until melted and smooth, about 5 minutes total. Towards the end, check every 20 to 30 seconds. Stir in 2½ cups candy and spread evenly in same parchment-lined baking pan; sprinkle with remaining ½ cup candy. Refrigerate about 1 hour or until firm. Break into pieces.

NOTE   For thinner bark, use a sheet pan instead of a 13×9-inch baking pan.

TROPICAL DUMP CAKE

MAKES 12 TO 16 SERVINGS

1 can (20 ounces) crushed pineapple, undrained

1 can (15 ounces) peach slices in light syrup, undrained

1 package (about 15 ounces) yellow cake mix

½ cup (1 stick) butter, cut into thin slices

1 cup packed brown sugar

½ cup flaked coconut

½ cup chopped pecans

1. Preheat oven to 350°F. Spray 13×9-inch baking pan with nonstick cooking spray.

2. Spread pineapple and peaches in prepared pan. Top with cake mix, spreading evenly. Top with butter in single layer, covering cake mix as much as possible. Sprinkle with brown sugar, coconut and pecans.

3. Bake 40 to 45 minutes or until toothpick inserted into center of cake comes out clean. Cool at least 15 minutes before serving.

CHOCOLATE PEANUT CRUNCH

MAKES ABOUT ¾ POUND

1 cup milk chocolate chips

½ cup semisweet chocolate chips

2 tablespoons corn syrup

1 tablespoon shortening

½ cup unsalted roasted peanuts

2 teaspoons vanilla

1. Spray 8-inch square baking pan with nonstick cooking spray.

2. Melt milk and semisweet chocolate chips with corn syrup and shortening in small heavy saucepan over low heat, stirring constantly.

3. Stir in peanuts and vanilla. Spread in prepared pan, distributing peanuts evenly. Refrigerate until firm. Break into pieces.

SEVEN-LAYER DESSERT

Makes 12 to 18 bars

½ cup (1 stick) butter, melted

1 teaspoon vanilla

1 cup graham cracker crumbs

1 cup butterscotch chips

1 cup chocolate chips

1 cup shredded coconut

1 cup nuts

1 can (14 ounces) sweetened condensed milk

1. Preheat oven to 350°F.

2. Pour butter into 13×9-inch baking pan. Add vanilla. Sprinkle cracker crumbs over butter. Layer butterscotch chips over crumbs, followed by chocolate chips, coconut and nuts. Pour condensed milk over all.

3. Bake 25 minutes or until lightly browned. Cool completely in pan on wire rack.

WHITE CHOCOLATE TRIANGLES

MAKES 6 DOZEN TRIANGLES

 1 cup white chocolate chips

½ cup sweetened condensed
   milk

½ cup chopped pecans,
   toasted*

½ (9-ounce) package
   chocolate wafers,
   crushed*

*To toast pecans, spread in single layer
in medium skillet. Cook over medium-
low heat 2 to 3 minutes or until lightly
toasted, stirring frequently.*

1. Grease 8-inch square baking pan.

2. Combine white chocolate chips and condensed milk in medium saucepan; cook and stir over low heat until chips are melted. Stir in pecans and crushed wafers.

3. Spread mixture in prepared pan; let stand until set. Cut into 36 squares; cut squares in half to form triangles. Store tightly covered in refrigerator; serve cold or at room temperature.

CHOCOLATE RAMEN FUDGE

MAKES 18 SERVINGS

1 package (12 ounces) semisweet chocolate chips

1 can (14 ounces) sweetened condensed milk

1 package (3 ounces) ramen noodles, any flavor, crumbled*

2 tablespoons butter, softened

1 teaspoon vanilla

Discard seasoning packet.

1. Line 8-inch square baking pan with foil, extending foil over edges of pan.

2. Place chocolate chips in medium microwavable bowl. Microwave on HIGH 1 minute; stir. Repeat heating and stirring at 30-second intervals until completely melted. Stir in condensed milk, crumbled noodles, butter and vanilla.

3. Spread mixture evenly in prepared pan. Refrigerate 1 hour or until firm. Remove from pan; peel off foil. Cut into squares.

SPIKY PRETZEL BALLS

MAKES ABOUT 3 DOZEN COOKIES

2 cups slightly crushed thin pretzel sticks

1 package (about 16 ounces) carrot or spice cake mix

2 eggs

5 tablespoons butter, melted

1 cup chow mein noodles

1 cup mini semisweet chocolate chips

1 cup butterscotch or peanut butter chips

1. Preheat oven to 350°F. Spray cookie sheets with nonstick cooking spray. Place pretzels in shallow bowl.

2. Combine cake mix, eggs and butter in large bowl until well blended. Stir in chow mein noodles, chocolate chips and butterscotch chips.

3. Shape dough into 1-inch balls; roll in pretzels, pressing firmly to adhere. Place 1 inch apart on prepared cookie sheets.

4. Bake 14 minutes or until cookies are no longer shiny. Cool on cookie sheets 5 minutes. Remove to wire racks; cool completely.

INDEX

METRIC CONVERSION CHART

VOLUME MEASUREMENTS (dry)

$\frac{1}{8}$ teaspoon = 0.5 mL
$\frac{1}{4}$ teaspoon = 1 mL
$\frac{1}{2}$ teaspoon = 2 mL
$\frac{3}{4}$ teaspoon = 4 mL
1 teaspoon = 5 mL
1 tablespoon = 15 mL
2 tablespoons = 30 mL
$\frac{1}{4}$ cup = 60 mL
$\frac{1}{3}$ cup = 75 mL
$\frac{1}{2}$ cup = 125 mL
$\frac{2}{3}$ cup = 150 mL
$\frac{3}{4}$ cup = 175 mL
1 cup = 250 mL
2 cups = 1 pint = 500 mL
3 cups = 750 mL
4 cups = 1 quart = 1 L

VOLUME MEASUREMENTS (fluid)

1 fluid ounce (2 tablespoons) = 30 mL
4 fluid ounces ($\frac{1}{2}$ cup) = 125 mL
8 fluid ounces (1 cup) = 250 mL
12 fluid ounces (1$\frac{1}{2}$ cups) = 375 mL
16 fluid ounces (2 cups) = 500 mL

WEIGHTS (mass)

$\frac{1}{2}$ ounce = 15 g
1 ounce = 30 g
3 ounces = 90 g
4 ounces = 120 g
8 ounces = 225 g
10 ounces = 285 g
12 ounces = 360 g
16 ounces = 1 pound = 450 g

DIMENSIONS

$\frac{1}{16}$ inch = 2 mm
$\frac{1}{8}$ inch = 3 mm
$\frac{1}{4}$ inch = 6 mm
$\frac{1}{2}$ inch = 1.5 cm
$\frac{3}{4}$ inch = 2 cm
1 inch = 2.5 cm

OVEN TEMPERATURES

250°F = 120°C
275°F = 140°C
300°F = 150°C
325°F = 160°C
350°F = 180°C
375°F = 190°C
400°F = 200°C
425°F = 220°C
450°F = 230°C

BAKING PAN SIZES

Utensil	Size in Inches/Quarts	Metric Volume	Size in Centimeters
Baking or Cake Pan (square or rectangular)	8×8×2	2 L	20×20×5
	9×9×2	2.5 L	23×23×5
	12×8×2	3 L	30×20×5
	13×9×2	3.5 L	33×23×5
Loaf Pan	8×4×3	1.5 L	20×10×7
	9×5×3	2 L	23×13×7
Round Layer Cake Pan	8×1½	1.2 L	20×4
	9×1½	1.5 L	23×4
Pie Plate	8×1¼	750 mL	20×3
	9×1¼	1 L	23×3
Baking Dish or Casserole	1 quart	1 L	—
	1½ quart	1.5 L	—
	2 quart	2 L	—